Object Lessons
for Family Devotions

Object Lessons Series

Bess, C. W., *Children's Object Sermons for the Seasons,* 1026-8

Bess, C. W., *Object-Centered Children's Sermons,* 0734-8

Bess, C. W., *Sparkling Object Sermons for Children,* 0824-7

Bess, C. W., & Roy DeBrand, *Bible-Centered Object Sermons for Children,* 0886-7

Biller, Tom & Martie, *Simple Object Lessons for Children,* 0793-3

Bruinsma, Sheryl, *Easy-to-Use Object Lessons,* 0832-8

Bruinsma, Sheryl, *More Object Lessons for Very Young Children,* 1075-6

Bruinsma, Sheryl, *New Object Lessons,* 0775-7

Bruinsma, Sheryl, *Object Lessons for Every Occasion,* 0994-4

Bruinsma, Sheryl, *Object Lessons for Special Days,* 0920-0

Bruinsma, Sheryl, *Object Lessons for Very Young Children,* 0956-1

Bruinsma, Sheryl, *Object Lessons Using Children's Toys,* 5695-0

Claassen, David, *Object Lessons for a Year,* 2514-1

Connelly, H. W., *47 Object Lessons for Youth Programs,* 2314-9

Coombs, Robert, *Concise Object Sermons for Children,* 2541-9

Coombs, Robert, *Enlightening Object Lessons for Children,* 2567-2

Cooper, Charlotte, *50 Object Stories for Children,* 2523-0

Cross, Luther, *Easy Object Stories,* 2502-8

Cross, Luther, *Object Lessons for Children,* 2315-7

Cross, Luther, *Story Sermons for Children,* 2328-9

DeJonge, Joanne, *All-Occasion Object Lessons,* 5690-X

DeJonge, Joanne, *More Object Lessons from Nature,* 3004-8

DeJonge, Joanne, *Object Lessons from Nature,* 2989-9

DeJonge, Joanne, *Object Lessons from Pebbles and Paper Clips,* 5041-3

DeJonge, Joanne, *Object Lessons from Your Home and Yard,* 3026-9

Edstrom, Lois, *Contemporary Object Lessons for Children's Church,* 3432-9

Gebhardt, Richard, & Mark Armstrong, *Object Lessons from Science Experiments,* 3811-1

Godsey, Kyle, *Object Lessons about God,* 3841-3

Hendricks, William, *Object Lessons Based on Bible Characters,* 4373-5

Hendricks, William, & Merle Den Bleyker, *Object Lessons from Sports and Games,* 4134-1

Hendricks, William, & Merle Den Bleyker, *Object Lessons That Teach Bible Truths,* 4172-4

Loeks, Mary, *Object Lessons for Children's Worship,* 5584-9

McDonald, Roderick, *Successful Object Sermons,* 6270-5

Runk, Wesley, *Object Lessons from the Bible,* 7698-6

Squyres, Greg, *Simple Object Lessons for Young Children,* 8330-3

Sullivan, Jessie, *Object Lessons and Stories for Children's Church,* 8037-1

Sullivan, Jessie, *Object Lessons with Easy-to-Find Objects,* 8190-4

Trull, Joe, *40 Object Sermons for Children,* 8831-3

Object Lessons
for Family Devotions

Sheryl Bruinsma

Baker Books

A Division of Baker Book House Co
Grand Rapids, Michigan 49516

Published by Baker Books
a division of Baker Book House Company
P.O. Box 6287, Grand Rapids, MI 49516-6287

Printed in the United States of America

Library of Congress Cataloging-in-Publication Data
Bruinsma, Sheryl.
    Object lessons for family devotions / Sheryl Bruinsma.
      p. cm.—(Object lessons series)
      ISBN 0-8010-5762-0 (pbk.)
    1. Family—Prayer-books and devotions—English. 2. Children—Prayer-books and devotions—English. 3. Christian education of children. 4. Object-teaching. I. Title. II. Series.
BV255.B74 1997
249—dc21   97-1659

For current information about all releases from Baker Book House, visit our web site:

                http://www.bakerbooks.com

Contents

Introduction

How well I remember sitting around the dinner table while my father read from the big Bible. My brother and I would kick each other under the table and wind up getting into trouble for giggling. Sometimes I would think about what I would be doing after dinner, or I would make roads in my leftover mashed potatoes. I do not remember ever interacting with what my father was reading. I just patiently endured our family devotions.

It is for this reason that I wrote this book. Family devotions should be a time when children are learning and participating. The text of this book was written in a way so that children can interact with the material. Children respond to questions asked. Activities are suggested to involve them and reinforce the story or concept. It is recommended that each time of devotions includes shared prayer.

This book is dedicated to drawing family members closer together through the study of God's Word so that the love of God and of each other forms a bond between them.

1

The Flood

Scripture: The flood continued for forty days, and the water became deep enough for the boat to float (Gen. 7:17).

Entire Text: Genesis 6:9–16; 7:11–22

Objects: A large bowl (preferably glass); small toys that will not float to represent people, animals, and objects covered by the flood; a toy boat or an object that will float to represent the boat such as a paper cup or a piece of wood; and water.

Long ago God looked at the people living on the earth and thought to himself, "These people are not at all the way they should be. Look at the terrible things they are doing—lying, cheating, stealing, even killing each other. They think about evil all the time. This cannot go on. I have to do something. I am going to send a flood to cover up and wash away all this evil.

"Now there *is* a good family down there—Noah and his wife and three sons. I will tell them to build a big boat with a roof on it so that the rain will roll off. Then I will tell Noah to take two of every kind of animal onto this big boat. That way when the flood is over, the animals can have babies and soon there will be many animals on the earth again."

So God told Noah what to do. Noah, being a good person who trusted God, did just what God said. Building such a big boat when there didn't seem to be a reason for it was a big test of Noah's faith. But he did it! And he loaded the boat with two of each kind of animal too.

Then the rain started. It was the heaviest rain Noah had ever seen. There was water everywhere! Noah and his family looked out the windows at the terrible rain. They were really happy that they had made a boat just as God had said.

The rain didn't stop. It kept raining and raining and soon Noah and his family felt the boat begin to move. That must have frightened them. Then they realized that the boat was floating on the water.

It rained for forty days and forty nights. The water went higher than the highest mountains. The boat with Noah and his family and the animals rose higher and higher. It floated on top of the water. God had saved Noah and his family.

God said he would never again send a flood like that one, but he still watches the people on earth. When he looks at our family, does he see one that would deserve to build a boat?

Activity: Retell the story by having the children put the "earth people and objects" into the bowl. Place a representation of a boat on top. Add water so that the boat will float to the top of the bowl.

2

Lot's Selfish Choice

Scripture: So Lot chose the whole Jordan Valley for himself and moved away toward the east. That is how the two men parted (Gen. 13:11).

Entire Text: Genesis 13:5–13

Object: A favorite dessert. By hollowing out the bottom of a piece of dessert, make one appear larger but in reality contain a smaller portion. Save the dessert for after the story. (You may wish to have the children choose their dessert before the story but wait to eat it.)

In Bible times, many people owned sheep and goats and cattle. These animals needed to graze on grass and drink water from lakes or streams. Abram and his nephew Lot owned animals. The problem was Abram and Lot had so many sheep and goats and cattle that there was not enough grass for all the animals to eat, and when the animals were thirsty, it became too crowded at the watering places.

The men who took care of Abram's animals and the men who took care of Lot's animals began to argue. They argued about who was at the watering place first. They argued about whose turn it was. They argued about who would get a certain area of grass. Do you know what happens when people begin to argue like this?

Abram was a man who loved God. He went to talk to Lot. He said, "This isn't right. We are relatives. Our men shouldn't be arguing. There must be a way to solve our problem. We will have to separate." Even back then they knew it was better to separate than to quarrel. We still send children to their rooms to separate them so that they cannot fight.

Abram was a generous man. He told Lot to look around and choose whatever part of the land he wanted. So Lot looked. He looked at rocky land and sandy land and land with some grass. But what he really liked was the Jordan Valley. The Jordan Valley had plenty of water because a river ran right through it. The valley was beautiful and green. So Lot chose the whole Jordan Valley for himself. He chose the biggest and the best. The problem was that he camped near the wicked city of Sodom. Soon he moved into Sodom. This led to all kinds of problems for Lot. Once he was even captured by an enemy and Abram had to go and rescue him. Lot did not make a good choice. He made a selfish one. Do you ever make selfish choices? Is it selfish to want to be first all the time? Is it selfish to always want the biggest piece?

Activity: Eat the dessert. Discuss the wisdom of the children's dessert choices based on the outcome.

3

Lot's Wife Looks Back

Scripture: Then one of the angels said, "Run for your lives! Don't look back and don't stop in the valley. Run to the hills, so that you won't be killed." . . . But Lot's wife looked back and was turned into a pillar of salt (Gen. 19:17, 26).

Entire Text: Genesis 19:12–29

Objects: Table salt, a cup, and water.

Lot was living in Sodom with his wife and his two daughters and their husbands. Sodom was a terrible place where people were mean to each other and did every bad thing they could think of. Lot knew better. He shouldn't have stayed living there. If you were in a place where people were doing all kinds of bad things, would you stay?

Two angels came to Lot and said, "Tell everyone in your family that they have to get out of here in a hurry because God has sent us to destroy this bad place."

Lot was basically a good man, even if he had made a bad choice to live in Sodom. He did just what the angels said. He told his wife and his daughters and their husbands that they had to leave right away. Do you know what the husbands of his daughters did? They laughed at Lot. They thought he was playing a joke on them. Can you imagine that? It's like staying in the middle of the road when someone tells you a car is coming.

So the angels took Lot and his wife and daughters by the hand and rushed them out of the city. One of the angels said, "Run for your lives! Don't look back and don't stop or you won't make it."

They were running for their lives when Lot's wife began to think about her beautiful things being left behind in Sodom. She wanted one last look at the place she had lived. She was curious about what was happening to it. Do you think she should look back?

Well, Lot's wife did look back, and do you know what happened to her? She turned into a pillar of salt. Lot and his two daughters had to run to safety without her.

Do you sometimes do things you are told not to do? Are you tempted to do wrong things when you think nobody is looking?

Activity: Pour regular table salt into a cup. Sprinkle it with a few drops of water and mix until the salt becomes moist. It can then be mounded like wet sand. When dry it will retain its shape. Have the children make a figure out of the moistened salt and retell the story of what happened to Lot's wife.

4

Jacob's Dream

Scripture: And he [Jacob] dreamed that there was a ladder set up on the earth, and the top of it reached to heaven; and behold, the angels of God were ascending and descending on it! (Gen. 28:12 RSV).

Entire Text: Genesis 28:10–22

Objects: Sheets of paper and scissors.

Jacob, a man who loved God, was going to a faraway city to find a wife. His mother wanted him to marry a nice girl from her people, one who would also love God. Back in Jacob's time, there were no cars to drive. It was a long, hard, hot trip by foot or riding on an animal. There were also no motels for Jacob to sleep in along the way. He simply made camp, found a place to stretch out, and used a stone for a pillow. That doesn't sound very comfortable, but I guess he didn't mind.

While Jacob was sleeping, he dreamed that he saw a ladder stretching way up into heaven. Angels were going up and going down on this ladder. It must have been an awesome sight. Then God spoke to Jacob. He told Jacob that he would have many children and grandchildren and that through him God would bless all nations. God said that he would be with Jacob and protect him and always keep his promises to him.

Jacob had a guilty conscience. He had tricked his father into giving him the blessing that belonged to his brother. He knew he didn't deserve all this from God. When he woke up, he said, "What a terrifying place this is." Feeling guilty about things we have done can make us feel scared.

I'm glad God doesn't just give us what we deserve. He will always love us, protect us, care for us, and give us his blessing. Thank you, God.

> **Activity:** Roll a piece of paper. Cut a section out of the middle. Unroll the paper and a ladder will be formed. With a little help or practice, the children will enjoy making paper ladders and retelling the story of Jacob.

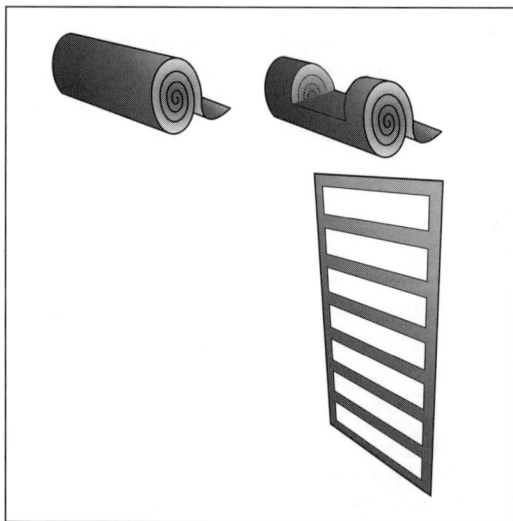

Jacob Is Tricked

Scripture: Not until the next morning did Jacob discover that it [his new wife] was Leah. He went to Laban and said, "Why did you do this to me? I worked to get Rachel. Why have you tricked me?" (Gen. 29:25).

Entire Text: Genesis 29:15–30

Objects: Table salt, sugar, a salt shaker, and a sugar bowl.

After Jacob's dream about the ladder, he continued on his way to find a wife. When he got close to where he was going, he asked some shepherds if they knew his Uncle Laban. They said, "Yes, we know him. This is his daughter Rachel coming now with his flock." Jacob was very happy to meet Rachel. She was quite beautiful.

Jacob stayed with his Uncle Laban and worked for him. After a month, Laban said, "How can I pay you for working for me?"

Jacob by now was in love with the beautiful Rachel and said, "I will work for you for seven years if I can marry Rachel."

Laban was happy that Rachel and Jacob were in love, but he had a problem. Rachel had an older sister, Leah.

Where Laban lived, older sisters were to be married first. At least he had seven years to find Leah a husband.

Rachel and Jacob waited the seven years to be married. Finally the time arrived and there was a big wedding. In those days, a bride wore heavy veils over her face so that her husband could not see her until after they were married.

When Jacob awoke the next morning, he was so happy that he was finally married to Rachel. He rolled over to look at his bride, but he saw that it was Leah. What a terrible trick Uncle Laban had played on Jacob.

Jacob got up and went to Uncle Laban and said, "Why did you do this to me? I worked to get Rachel. Why have you tricked me?"

Uncle Laban said, "Leah still wasn't married and she had to be married first. Wait a week and I will give you Rachel also. However, you have to promise to work for me for another seven years."

Jacob promised, but he always loved Rachel more than Leah, and he never got over being tricked.

Have you ever played a mean trick on somebody?

Activity: Put salt in the sugar bowl and sugar in the salt shaker. Have the children put some sugar from the salt shaker or salt from the sugar bowl on their food or into their hand to taste. Discuss the difference between a little joke that will help them remember the story and a mean trick such as the one played on Jacob.

Joseph's Coat

Scripture: Jacob loved Joseph more than all his other sons, because he had been born to him when he was old. He made a long robe with full sleeves for him. When his brothers saw that their father loved Joseph more than he loved them, they hated their brother so much that they would not speak to him in a friendly manner (Gen. 37:3–4).

Entire Text: Genesis 37:1–24

Object: Any object that all the children would like to hold. Give the object to one of the children to hold while the lesson is read.

Sometimes things happen that are not a person's fault. The story of Joseph and his coat is one example.

Jacob had two wives. Rachel was the one he loved very much and had wanted to marry. For many, many years Rachel wanted desperately to have a baby. Jacob had other children, but he wanted Rachel to have a baby also. Finally, when Jacob was old, Rachel had her first baby. It was a boy, and they called him Joseph. Jacob loved this baby more than any of his other children because he and Rachel had wanted a baby for a very long time. Joseph's older brothers were jealous of all the attention Joseph was getting.

As Joseph grew older, the jealousy became worse. Jacob loved Joseph so much that he gave Joseph a special coat. It was very beautiful. It was long and had full sleeves. This made Joseph's brothers angry. That was a bad way to feel. It made the brothers mean. They would not even talk to Joseph in a friendly way.

Brothers and sisters often fight. They may even say unkind things to each other, but they only mean them for a little while. Do you ever fight with your brother or sister? You may get mad, but you get over it. When brothers and sisters are fighting, it makes everyone sad or angry. Everyone is happy when the fight is over and there is friendliness again.

This didn't happen with Joseph and his brothers. The brothers were jealous and angry and mean to Joseph. They never had a nice word to say to him. It wasn't even Joseph's fault.

One day Joseph's brothers were late getting home, so Joseph's father sent him to find out if anything was wrong. When Joseph's brothers saw him coming, they said, "This is our chance. Let's kill Joseph and throw his body into a dry well. We'll say that a wild animal killed him."

One brother named Reuben, who was not as bad as the rest, said, "Don't kill him. Just take his coat and throw him into the well." He planned to come back later and rescue Joseph from the well. However, when Reuben was gone, the other brothers sold Joseph as a slave. When Reuben came back to get Joseph, he was gone.

Then the brothers took Joseph's coat, dipped it in goat blood, and brought it back to their father so that he would think Joseph was dead. You can imagine how upset Jacob was! Do you think Jacob loved his other sons more after he thought Joseph was dead? Can you imagine anyone being so mean to their brother? Are you mean to your brother or sister?

Activity: Discuss with the children how they felt about holding or not holding the object. Talk about how the children should love their siblings even if one gets to do something the others do not.

7

Baby Moses' Basket

Scripture: But when she could not hide him any longer, she took a basket made of reeds and covered it with tar to make it watertight. She put the baby in it and then placed it in the tall grass at the edge of the river (Exod. 2:3).

Entire Text: Exodus 1:21–2:10

Objects: A flat-bottomed basket, a container of water large enough to hold the basket, and Vaseline.

Long ago, God's people lived in a country that was not their own. They had to do everything the rulers of that country said. The king of that country was afraid because God's people were becoming strong and increasing in number. He was so afraid that he did something terrible. The king commanded that every baby boy born to God's people had to be thrown into the river. Do you know what happens when you throw a newborn baby boy into a river? Yes, he drowns. Wasn't that a terrible thing?

One brave mother looked at her beautiful little baby boy named Moses and said, "I can't possibly have this wonderful little baby thrown into the river. I am going to hide him." Well, this worked for a few months, but it became difficult to hide the baby as he got older. The mother came up with a new plan. She decided to put Moses in a basket and float the basket in the river where the princess went to bathe. She hoped the princess would find her baby and would want her cute little boy to live.

The mother was very smart. She got a basket that was the right size for her baby. The mother put tar on the outside of the basket to make sure that the water could not get in. She put her baby in the basket and placed it in the tall grass that grew by the side of the river. Then she told the baby's big sister to keep watch to see what happened. The mother trusted God to take care of her little baby.

Do you know what happened to Moses? The princess *did* find him. She also felt sorry for him and wanted to help him. The baby's sister came over to the princess and offered to find somebody to help her take care of the baby. Do you know who she found? Of course, it was the baby's own mother. The mother had trusted God to take care of the baby, and now the baby had been given back to her to take care of. Her baby boy was not drowned in the river. When he was older, Moses was adopted by the princess and raised in the king's palace. Moses' mother trusted God, and God took care of her baby. Do you trust God to take care of you?

Activity: Put Vaseline on the outside of the basket to make it watertight. Float the basket and act out the story. Talk about ways the children can trust God.

23

8

Samson

Scripture: She kept on asking him, day after day. He got so sick and tired of her bothering him about it that he finally told her the truth. "My hair has never been cut," he said (Judg. 16:16–17).

Entire Text: Judges 16:4–22

Objects: Plates and napkins (or placemats).

Samson was the strongest man who ever lived. He was so strong that one day some men wanted to catch him and kill him. They locked a gate so that he couldn't get away. Samson pulled the heavy gate and its posts right out of the wall and carried it away on his shoulders. He was so strong that nobody could stop him.

Samson fell in love with a woman named Delilah. She was very beautiful, but Samson knew he could not trust her. She begged him to tell her why he was so strong. He made up a story and told her that he could be caught if someone tied him with special ropes. While he was sleeping, Delilah tied him up. Then the men came to catch him. Samson broke the ropes and got away. This kind of thing happened several times. Samson knew he could not trust Delilah.

Samson was strong, but he was not always smart. Instead of leaving Delilah, he stayed with her. She kept pestering him to tell her why he was strong. She whined and said, "If you really love me, you will tell me." Finally, Samson told her that he was strong because his hair had never been cut. This was the truth, and Delilah knew it. She sent for the men who wanted to catch him, and she had his hair cut off while he was sleeping.

Samson woke up, and he knew that God had left him. His hair was cut, and he had lost his strength. The men caught him and put his eyes out and took him away. What do you think is better, to be smart or to be strong? If you are smart and you do what God wants you to do, does that make you strong?

Activity: Put a plate on a napkin or placemat. Ask the children to move the plate without touching it. In order to move the plate, they will have to figure out (or be told) to move the placemat or napkin. Discuss the fact that being very strong would not be enough to move the plate without touching it.

9

God Forgives Samson

Scripture: Then Samson prayed, "Sovereign LORD, please remember me; please, God, give me my strength just this one time more . . ." (Judg. 16:28).

Entire Text: Judges 16:23–31

Objects: Building blocks.

Do you remember how foolish Samson was when he told Delilah why he was so strong? He knew she would try to take his strength so that the men who wanted to kill him could catch him. He got carried away and told her anyway. The men caught him and put his eyes out, but they did not kill him. They liked seeing Samson without his strength. They made him push the big grinding stone in the prison. They laughed at him and made fun of the man who used to be the strongest man in the world.

God had not forgotten Samson, though. While Samson worked in the prison pushing the heavy grinding stone, his muscles grew stronger. His hair began to grow back. Samson must have been very sorry for what he did. While he was blind and in prison, he always remembered God.

One day the men who caught him were celebrating their own made-up god, who is not the one true God. They said, "Remember that fellow Samson whom we caught. Let's bring him over here so we can laugh at him and make fun of him. Our made-up god is stronger than he is. He used to be so strong. Just look at him now."

Samson was led by a little boy because he had no eyes to see where he was going. The little boy put Samson's hands on the columns that held up the building so Samson could lean on them. Then Samson prayed for God to give him back his strength one more time so he could destroy this bad place and the men who were so mean to him and who worshiped their made-up god.

Do you think God heard Samson's prayer? Do you think God hears your prayers? Do you think God forgave Samson and gave him back his strength? Do you think God forgives you and makes you the same again? Do you think Samson was strong enough to bring down the whole building? The answer to all these questions is yes!

Activity: With the blocks, construct a building that is supported by columns on the first level. Have the children demonstrate how Samson could move the columns and bring down the building.

10

David and Goliath

Scripture: David answered, "You are coming against me with sword, spear, and javelin, but I come against you in the name of the LORD Almighty, the God of the Israelite armies, which you have defied" (1 Sam. 17:45).

Entire Text: 1 Samuel 17:31–51

Objects: Five smooth stones and a measuring tape to measure over nine feet tall.

Once there was a war. It was between the Philistines and the people of God called the Israelites. The men were lined up to fight each other with swords and spears when one of the Philistines stepped forward. He said, "Choose someone to fight me. Whoever wins will make the others their slaves. Here I am. I dare you to pick someone to fight me."

This might not have been so bad if the man had not been Goliath. Goliath was over nine feet tall. He wore heavy armor and had a thick, heavy spear. Everyone knew they could not get close enough to this giant to fight him. They knew they would surely die if they tried. They were all so frightened at the thought of fighting this huge, strong giant that they were shaking in their boots.

Every morning and every evening for forty days Goliath came forward and dared them to fight him. Finally, one brave shepherd boy named David said, "I'm not afraid of this giant, Goliath. Let me fight him."

They said, "How can you fight him? You are just a boy. You have been a shepherd and do not know how to be a soldier."

David stood up straight and tall and told them, "I killed lions and bears to take care of my sheep. If God can save me from lions and bears, he can save me from this Philistine." That was very brave of David. He truly believed that God would take care of him.

The Israelite soldiers tried to make David wear heavy armor, but he couldn't walk in it. Instead, he picked up his shepherd's stick and five smooth stones from the stream. With his slingshot ready, he bravely went to face Goliath.

When Goliath saw David coming to fight him, he laughed at him and said, "Do you think I am a dog that you can chase me with a stick? I curse your God and I will tear your body into pieces and feed them to the birds and animals."

David did not run away. He looked the giant in the eyes and said, "I come in the name of the Lord and it is I who will kill you." David took a stone and put it in his slingshot and hit Goliath on the forehead. The giant fell down dead.

David loved God with his whole heart, and God took care of David. Do you love God with your whole heart? Do you trust God to take care of you?

Activity: Measure the size of Goliath. Look at the size of the stones and the size of Goliath. Discuss how brave David was and how much he trusted God to help him.

11

Renewal

Scripture:
Create a pure heart in me, O God,
    and put a new and loyal spirit in me.
Help me to speak, Lord,
    and I will praise you (Ps. 51:10, 15).

Entire Text: Psalm 51:10–15

Objects: A dirty toy to clean or silver to polish,
soap and water or silver polish.

The psalms, or songs, are like poems. We have lost
the tunes because they were not written down. Many
people today use the words and make up new tunes. It
is a good idea to make up songs about God and how
much we love him. This makes us happy, and it makes
God happy.

Something else that makes us happy is being clean
or like new. Do you like how you feel after you are just
out of the bathtub and wrapped in a big, warm towel?
Do you like to put on new clothes or play with a new
toy? Do you like the feeling of waking up in the morning feeling rested and ready to go?

David sings about this new feeling in the words of a
song: "Create a pure heart in me, O God, and put a new
and loyal spirit in me." What would a pure, or clean,

heart be like? Would it be mean or kind? Would it be loving or spiteful? Would it be lying or honest? Would it be patient or hateful? It is sometimes difficult for us to keep our hearts clean. We may find a little bit of jealousy dirt getting into our hearts along with some meanness sand and unkindness dust. This song is really a prayer for God to clean up the heart. Do you want God to clean your heart?

This song also says, "Help me to speak, Lord, and I will praise you." How wonderful to let God speak through us and help us say the right thing. God will help us sing and talk about him.

We talk about making New Year's resolutions. We say that on New Year's Day we will begin to show our clean heart by doing good things. We promise that we will speak the words God gives and be a better person. The problem with New Year's resolutions is that if one gets broken, the person says, "Well, that one is broken. I'll have to try again next year." What? Wait a whole year? That's not what our song means. Psalm 51 says we should sing and pray every day for a clean heart and for words to speak for God. Maybe we should change it from New Year's resolution to New Day's resolution. Are you willing to ask God to make you new each day?

Activity: Have the children clean a dirty toy (or polish tarnished silver) to show the newness of being clean.

31

12

Giving Thanks

Scripture:
Let us come before him with thanksgiving
and sing joyful songs of praise (Ps. 95:2).

Entire Text: Psalm 95:1–7

Objects: Sheets of paper and crayons or markers.

It doesn't need to be Thanksgiving for us to be thankful. God wants us to be thankful all the time. Being thankful is a way of praising God. When we are thankful, we are joyful. We are thinking about God and how great he is. We are happy that he is so good to us.

Being thankful also makes us happy because we are thinking about what we have, not grumbling about something we might not have. It helps us to think about the blessings God gives us. It keeps us from taking our homes and families for granted. It makes us stop and think about all the big things that are important in life and all the little extras we have.

Being thankful is a way of praying. It is talking to God and thanking him for the wonderful things he gives us. It is telling him that we understand and appreciate the way he takes care of our needs (not our *wants*, but our *needs*). It is telling him we love him because we care about all the things he does for us.

Being thankful can also be a way of singing. When the shepherd boy David wrote the songs called psalms, he sang to God. He wrote the words, "Let us come before him with thanksgiving and sing joyful songs of praise." When I was little, I used to sing, "Thank you, Lord, for saving my soul. Thank you, Lord, for making me whole. Thank you, Lord, for giving to me Thy great salvation so rich and free."

Activity: Have the children draw pictures of what they are thankful for and then hang the pictures on the refrigerator.

13

The Fiery Furnace

Scripture: Suddenly Nebuchadnezzar leaped to his feet in amazement. He asked his officials, "Didn't we tie up three men and throw them into the blazing furnace? . . . Then why do I see four men walking around in the fire?" he asked. . . . "They show no sign of being hurt—and the fourth one looks like an angel" (Dan. 3:24–25).

Entire Text: Daniel 3:1–30

Objects: Paper dolls (children can make these), rubbing alcohol and water (half and half mixture), matches, and tongs.

Daniel was a man who loved God. He had been chosen by the king of Babylon to be a ruler in his kingdom. The king also made Daniel's three friends, Shadrach, Meshach, and Abednego, important.

One day when Daniel was away, the king made a huge gold statue. Then the people had a big celebration. The people were told to bow down and worship the gold statue or be thrown into a burning furnace. Well, the people didn't want to be thrown into the burning furnace, so they bowed down and worshiped the statue. That is, all the people except Daniel's friends Shadrach,

Meshach, and Abednego. They loved God and knew that they should not worship anyone but God.

Some people who were jealous of the three friends went to tell the king. Of course, the king was angry. He called the three friends and said, "Shadrach, Meshach, and Abednego, my gold statue is god and you must worship it. If you do not, you will be thrown into the furnace right away. Do you think your God will save you?"

The men replied that whether they lived or died, they would not worship the gold statue as god. This made the king even angrier, and he ordered that the furnace be made seven times hotter than usual. Then the three men were tied up and led to the furnace. The furnace was so hot that the guards who had to throw the three men into the furnace were burned up themselves.

The king went to take a look at Shadrach, Meshach, and Abednego. He was still angry and wanted to see them burning up. He was so surprised to find the men actually walking around in the fire. He was even more amazed to find four men alive in the fire. He yelled, "They are not tied up, and they don't look like they are even hurt. That fourth one over there looks like an angel."

The king ran to the door of the furnace and told them to come out. "Your God is the true one," he said. "Praise the God of Shadrach, Meshach, and Abednego, who rescued them from the fire because they served and trusted him."

You are not likely to be put in a furnace because you did not obey a ruler, but there may be times when you will need to take a stand for what you believe. If you hear someone swearing, what will you do? If you see someone picking on another person, what will you do?

If you know someone is stealing, what will you do? When people see you, will they be able to tell that you have a great God?

Activity: Wet paper figures in the half alcohol and half water mixture. Parents can hold the figures with tongs and light them. The alcohol will burn off because it burns at a lower temperature, leaving the figures unharmed.

14

Daniel in the Lions' Den

Scripture: Daniel answered, "May Your Majesty live forever! God sent his angel to shut the mouths of the lions so that they would not hurt me. He did this because he knew that I was innocent and because I have not wronged you, Your Majesty" (Dan. 6:21–22).

Entire Text: Daniel 6:1–28

Objects: Stuffed animals and a toy or doll to represent Daniel.

Daniel was a man who loved God. He always did his work well. He never lied or cheated or forgot to do what he was supposed to do. Because of this, the king made him head ruler in charge of the whole empire. The men who were now under Daniel did not like this one bit. They got together and said, "We have to find something wrong with Daniel so we can get rid of him." They watched Daniel carefully, but he always did his job well.

They gave up trying to find something wrong with Daniel and decided to make something up. They went to the king and said, "Oh, King, you are so wise and wonderful. Everyone should honor you. You should make it a very firm law that for thirty days nobody can ask any god or another man for anything. They may only ask you. You are so great. People should spend thirty days knowing that only you can answer all their needs. And just to make sure that everybody does this, make it a law also that they will be thrown into a pit of lions if they do not do it." They kept saying things like that to the king until he agreed to make it a very firm law.

The men did this to trick Daniel because they knew that he prayed to God every day. They listened at his window, and when they heard him pray, they went running to the king. "Oh, King, Daniel did not respect your law. We heard him pray to his God. You know what has to happen."

The king was very upset. "Oh, why did I ever agree to this silly law? I listened to all of their sweet talk."

The king had to have Daniel put into the pit of lions. He said to Daniel, "May your God rescue you." He felt so sorry for Daniel that he could not sleep that night. At dawn, the king got up and rushed to the pit. "Daniel, Daniel, did your God save you?" he called.

The king was overjoyed when he heard Daniel talking. "May your Majesty live forever," Daniel answered, because that's the way you talk to kings. "God sent an angel to shut the mouths of the lions so they could not hurt me. He did this because I never did anything to wrong you." The king commanded everyone to respect Daniel's God and made Daniel ruler again. He was happy to have such an honest and loyal worker. Are you a good worker?

Activity: Using the stuffed animals and the figure, have the children recreate Daniel's rescue from the lions. Stress how Daniel was rewarded for being faithful to God and a diligent worker.

15

Jesus Is Born

Scripture: When the angels went away from them back into heaven, the shepherds said to one another, "Let's go to Bethlehem and see this thing that has happened, which the Lord has told us." So they hurried off and found Mary and Joseph and saw the baby lying in the manger (Luke 2:15–16).

Entire Text: Luke 2:8–20

Object: Extra table setting for Jesus.

Up to this point, the stories told in this book came from the Old Testament. They were about things that happened before Jesus was born on this earth. In the Bible, after the Old Testament comes the New Testament. At the beginning of the New Testament, the baby Jesus was born. That was the beginning of many new and exciting things. Because it is such a wonderful story, we should think about it more than just at Christmas.

Close your eyes and imagine that it is dark. You are a shepherd and you are with your shepherd friends out in the field at night watching over your sheep. You are listening for any wild animals that might want to eat your sheep, especially the baby lambs. Suddenly an angel appears with a light so bright that you are scared to death.

Now imagine that the angel says, "Don't be afraid. I'm here to bring you some good news. In the city of David, your Savior was born. This will prove it to you: You will find the baby wrapped in cloths and lying in a manger."

Open your eyes and pretend to look at the other shepherds. What do you think you will do? Yes, I think you and your friends will run just as fast as you can. What will you find when you get there? A sweet, little baby Jesus lying in a manger. Do you think you will worship the baby? Do you think you will feel that he is a wonderful baby?

The shepherds actually got to see the baby in the manger. When they went away, they kept him in their hearts. We also keep Jesus in our hearts. That means we think about him, we pray to him, we sing and talk about him, and we love him. By setting a place for Jesus at our table, we show that he is here with us.

Activity: Make room at your table for Jesus. You might want to wrap a doll in a blanket. Children can pretend to be angels bringing the story to the shepherds.

16

Life-Giving Water

Scripture: Jesus answered, "Whoever drinks this water will get thirsty again, but whoever drinks the water that I will give him will never be thirsty again. The water that I will give him will become in him a spring which will provide him with life-giving water and give him eternal life" (John 4:13–14).

Entire Text: John 4:5–26

Objects: A glass of water for each family member, but don't let anyone have a drink during dinner.

One day Jesus was walking to Galilee. In those days, people usually walked when they wanted to go somewhere. They didn't have cars or buses. Jesus became very tired and thirsty and rested by a well. A Samaritan woman came along. Jews weren't supposed to speak to Samaritans. They certainly weren't allowed to use the same cups and bowls. The woman was surprised, therefore, when Jesus asked her for a drink, but she gave him one. Jesus knew better than to treat her differently just because she was a Samaritan.

Then Jesus said something very strange to her. He told her that he could give her life-giving water and that whoever drinks this life-giving water would never be thirsty again.

Think about it a minute. Is it possible to take a drink today and never get thirsty again? Jesus could have done it, but that is not what he meant. He meant that her soul, the part of her that thinks and feels, would be satisfied. When he said that he would give her life-giving water, he meant eternal life. He wanted to give the woman his spirit so that she would have a life filled with the love of God. Then her soul would not be thirsty, feel empty, or feel like it needed something ever again.

Deep down inside all of us is a place that only God can fill. It is like a thirst that only drinking can quench. God made us to know him, to love him, and to be filled with him. Your soul is thirsty for God.

Activity: Have each person take a drink and talk about how God satisfies body and soul.

17

Fishers of Men

Scripture: Jesus said to Simon, "Don't be afraid; from now on you will be catching men" (Luke 5:10).

Entire Text: Luke 5:1–11

Objects: Bowl of Cheerios or other cereal with holes that can be hooked, and a bent paper clip on a string.

When Jesus talked to people, they liked to crowd very close to him. Wouldn't you want to get close to Jesus if you were there? Once when Jesus was by the shore of a lake, he got closer and closer to the water as the crowd of people tried to get closer and closer to him. Jesus saw two fishing boats coming to shore. Jesus got into one of the boats and asked the owner, Simon, to push off a little from the shore. That way Jesus could talk to the people better, without getting wet!

When Jesus was finished talking, he told Simon to push the boat out farther and put the nets down to catch fish. "It's no use," Simon said. "We have been fishing all night and haven't caught a single fish." However, Simon did what Jesus said. The fishermen were amazed when they pulled up the nets and found they were filled with fish. There were so many fish that the nets began to break. The fishermen waved at their partners in the other boat and motioned for them to come out and help. When the men had pulled in all the fish, the two boats were so full that they began to sink. Imagine all those fish! Simon knew then that the Lord was in his boat.

The men were so amazed that they became frightened. Have you ever been so surprised by something that it scared you? Jesus had to tell the men not to be afraid. Then he told them that they would be fishers of men. What do you think he meant by that? He meant that they would tell everybody they met about Jesus. They would also go along with Jesus and help him talk to people. They would catch men with Jesus' love and power. Then these men (this meant women and children too) would be fished out of their ordinary lives and their old ways of doing things, which were not always good. The people would have a new and wonderful life following Jesus.

Activity: Fish for cereal and have the children explain in their own words what is meant by fishing for men.

18

The Blind Man

Scripture: He rubbed the mud on the man's eyes and told him, "Go and wash your face in the Pool of Siloam." . . . So the man went, washed his face, and came back seeing (John 9:6–7).

Entire Text: John 9:1–41

Objects: Scarves to cover the children's eyes.

As Jesus was walking along, he saw a man who had been born blind. Can you imagine what it would be like to be born blind? You wouldn't even know what color the sky is because you would never have seen it.

Jesus had disciples, or friends, with him. They asked Jesus, "Why was this man born blind? Was it his fault? Was it his parents' fault? Someone must have sinned."

Jesus answered that it is not always someone's fault when something bad happens. Sometimes bad things happen and nobody should be blamed. Sometimes good things can come out of bad things. In this case, Jesus was about to heal the blind man. He put mud on the man's eyes and told him to go wash it off. When the man did, he could see.

That was such a wonderful and unusual thing to have happen that the people standing around could not believe it. They said, "Is this the same man? No, he only looks like the man. He couldn't be the blind man."

So the man said, "Yes, I am the man." Then the people thought that maybe he hadn't really been blind, but too many people knew that he had been. They were very upset and did not want to believe that Jesus could do this, so they sent the man away.

When Jesus found out how they had treated the man, he went looking for him. Jesus said, "I came into the world so that the blind could see. It is also true that some people who think they see are really blind." What did Jesus mean when he said this? He meant that the people who were looking right at Jesus and did not see or want to see who he was were the blind ones. They could not see that Jesus was the Son of God. They did not have his love in their hearts. That made them blind to Jesus and to what really mattered. This also helps us know that we do not need to actually see Jesus to love him and to know that he is the powerful Son of God. We can "see" him with our hearts and our minds. Can you "see" Jesus?

Activity: While their eyes are covered, tell the children to picture Jesus smiling and looking lovingly at them.

19

The House on the Rock

Scripture: The rain poured down, the rivers flooded over, and the wind blew hard against that house. But it did not fall, because it was built on rock (Matt. 7:25).

Entire Text: Matthew 7:24–27

Objects: A cake pan, a pile of sand that will fit in the middle of it (sugar can be used if no sand is available), a rock, a small house or block to represent a house, and a pitcher of water. You will need to have the objects ready before reading the story.

Jesus wanted to tell the people to trust in him and not in the things around them, so he told the people a story. He told them that if people listen to his words and obey them, they are like a wise man who builds his house on a rock. [Have the children place the rock in the pan and the "house" on the rock.] When rain pours and the river floods and the wind blows, the house stays safely on the rock. [Have the children pour in the water.] This house is safe because the people trust in Jesus, who is like a rock—strong and sturdy.

Now, let's suppose that people know about Jesus and hear his words and don't believe them. They laugh and say, "I can take care of myself. Look at all the good stuff I have. Nothing can hurt me. I don't need God." Jesus told the people that these people are like the foolish man who built his house on the sand. [Empty the pan. Have the children place a pile of sand in the pan and place the "house" on the sand.] Let's see what happens to these people who think they don't need God. [Have the children pour in the water. Shake the pan slightly if needed.] Look! The house is being washed away.

Are you like the wise man who built his house on the rock or the foolish man who built his house on the sand?

Activity: Act out the story as it is told.

Clean the Inside First

Scripture: Blind Pharisee! Clean what is inside the cup first, and then the outside will be clean too! (Matt. 23:26).

Entire Text: Matthew 23:1–28

Objects: Two cups, one dirty on the inside and one dirty on the outside.

There was a group of people who were leaders during the time Jesus lived. These men thought they were better than everybody else. They sat in the best seats and wanted everyone to call them "Teacher." The gold in the temple was more important to them than the fact that the temple was the holy place of God. They followed the religious laws but did not bother with important things such as justice and mercy and honesty.

They were clean on the outside, but inside they were dirty and full of selfishness and greed. They were like a place for dead bodies that is beautiful on the outside but full of bones and decay on the inside.

Jesus was very angry with these men and had plenty to say to them. He said they did everything so that people would see them and would say how wonderful they were.

49

The point of following God is not so you can brag to other people, especially when you are bragging while at the same time you are being mean. The whole point of following God is so that you will have a better, cleaner inside. Your life is filled with love and goodness and kindness. That way you will *be* good, not just talk as if you are good. Do you like it when someone does something to you and then he or she says, "I didn't do it. I wouldn't do anything like that."

Look at the two cups. If you had to take a drink from one, which one would you choose? Being clean on the inside is the most important. Let's think about something else. When you put soap and water into a dirty cup and scrub it and then you rinse the cup off, the outside becomes clean also. Jesus knows that if your inside is clean and kind and pure, your outside will also be clean. What are you like on the inside?

Activity: Examine and discuss the cups. Which cup are you most like? Which cup would you rather be like?

21

The Lost Sheep

Scripture: "Suppose one of you has a hundred sheep and loses one of them—what does he do? He leaves the other ninety-nine sheep in the pasture and goes looking for the one that got lost until he finds it" (Luke 15:4).

Entire Text: Luke 15:1–7

Objects: Many small toys spread over the table.

One day the local religious men were grumbling. They were always trying to find fault with Jesus because they did not understand him. They had a list of laws. Their lives revolved around following these laws. Jesus was more interested in people than in silly laws. When Jesus went against a law, the religious men got upset. One law said that Jews could only talk to and eat with other Jews. The men grumbled and complained when Jesus talked to and ate with people who were not Jews.

Jesus often told people stories. We call them parables because they had a special meaning and taught a lesson. Jesus told the men a story about the Good Shepherd. In the story Jesus told, the Good Shepherd knew every one of his sheep, and he had a hundred of them. One day one sheep was missing. The Good Shepherd went out and looked and looked for that sheep. He looked until he found it. He was so happy and excited to find it that he carried it on his shoulders all the way home. When he got back, he called everyone to celebrate because he had found his lost sheep.

Then Jesus told the men that there will be more joy and excitement and celebrating in heaven over one lost sinner than there will be about the ninety-nine good people who were never in danger.

The deeper meaning to this story was that Jesus needed to talk to all people, not just the ones the men thought were good. It is much more exciting to find a lost sheep than one that was never in danger. Jesus knew that his message of salvation was for everyone. Whether you are one of the ninety-nine safe sheep or the one that is lost, Jesus will always love you.

Activity: While the children's eyes are closed, remove one of the objects from the table. See if the children can guess which one it is. Talk about how the Good Shepherd knew all one hundred sheep.

22

The Lost Son

Scripture: So he went to work for one of the citizens of that country, who sent him out to his farm to take care of the pigs. He wished he could fill himself with the bean pods the pigs ate, but no one gave him anything to eat (Luke 15:15–16).

Entire Text: Luke 15:11–24

Objects: Save the scraps from dinner and dump them all on a plate in an unappetizing manner.

Jesus wanted the people of his day to know why his message was for everyone, especially those who needed it the most. He told another story.

Once a man had two sons. The younger son was restless. He wasn't happy working in the fields. The son asked his father to give him his share of the property, and the son sold it. Then he took the money and went away. The father must have been very disappointed and upset. It was as if his son ran away from home.

The son was young and foolish. He wasted his money. He bought things he didn't need and tried to make himself look important to the people around him. He had friends when he had money, but when the money was gone, he was all alone. He was hungry, and he had to find a job. Do you remember that he did not want to work in the fields with his father and brother? Well, the only job he could get was to take care of pigs. Do you think that was a better job? He was willing to eat what the pigs ate, but no one gave him anything to eat.

The son was miserable and lonely. He realized that the hired workers of his father had plenty to eat, while he was starving. He was very sorry for selling his share of the property and for leaving his home. He wondered if his father missed him. Do you think his father missed him? Do you think his father wanted him back?

The young man said to himself, "I will go back to my father and tell him how sorry I am and beg him to hire me on as a worker. My life shall be much better. How foolish I was."

He got up and started walking back to his father. His father saw him coming while he was still a long way off. "Could that possibly be my son?" the father said. "Oh, what a wonderful day. My son is coming back." He ran to his son and hugged him and kissed him. "I am so happy that you are alive, my son. Welcome back."

The son said, "I have been so terrible. I should not even be called your son anymore." But the father was good to his long-lost son. He gave his son clothes and shoes so that he was once again dressed like the son of the owner. Then they had a big celebration.

Why did Jesus tell this story? He wants all his children safe in his loving care. Are you one of Jesus' children?

Activity: Show the plate of scraps and discuss how desperate the son must have been to be willing to eat what the pigs ate.

23

Walking on Water

Scripture: "Come!" answered Jesus. So Peter got out of the boat and started walking on the water to Jesus. But when he noticed the strong wind, he was afraid and started to sink down in the water. "Save me, Lord!" he cried. At once Jesus reached out and grabbed hold of him (Matt. 14:29–31).

Entire Text: Matthew 14:22–33

Objects: A bowl of water and plastic figures, preferably people, that will not float.

One day Jesus was with his disciples. He wanted to pray so he sent them out in the boat ahead of him. Jesus knew it was important to have time alone to pray to God.

It was very windy and the boat was tossing back and forth when Jesus was ready to join the disciples. It was early in the morning, probably still dark. Jesus didn't want to call the boat back so, being God, he simply stepped out on the water and began walking. When the disciples saw Jesus walking toward them on the water, they thought he was a ghost. They were terrified.

Jesus called out to them, "It is I. Don't be afraid." Then Peter, who was not one to let an opportunity go by, said, "Jesus, if it is really you, tell me to come out on the water to you."

Jesus told him to come. Peter swung his feet over the side of the boat. He must have really trusted Jesus to go out onto the water. He was doing it. He was really walking on the water. It was amazing. As long as he kept his eyes on Jesus, he could actually walk on the water.

But then Peter began to look around him. He noticed how bad the wind and the waves were. He looked down. Do you know what happened when he looked down? Yes, Peter began to sink. He called out to Jesus to save him. Jesus reached out and grabbed him. He told Peter that he was there for him. Jesus asked Peter why he began to doubt him.

That was a very good question. When we know how wonderful and powerful Jesus is, why do we doubt him? Having faith means that we will always trust Jesus to do what he says. Do you?

Activity: Drop the figures into the water. Discuss how Peter sank when he doubted Jesus. Have the children think of ways they can trust Jesus.

56

24

Jesus Loves the Little Children

Scripture: But Jesus called the children to him and said, "Let the children come to me and do not stop them, because the Kingdom of God belongs to such as these" (Luke 18:16).

Entire Text: Luke 18:15–17

Objects: A drinking glass that is too small for an adult's hand but that a child's hand will fit into, and a coin.

During the time when Jesus lived on earth, women and children were not considered important. Women stayed home to take care of the house, and children were supposed to do whatever they were told, including working much of the time. Because of this, mothers and children were not supposed to bother Jesus, especially when he was talking to a group of men.

One day Jesus was having an important conversation with not only men but the leaders of the men. Surely no one would try to interrupt them.

However, a group of mothers came up to where Jesus was talking. They knew that Jesus had done wonderful things and was a special person. They wanted him to put his hands on their children and bless them. They wanted their children to see firsthand the person everyone talked about.

When these mothers were trying to get close to Jesus, the disciples, Jesus' friends, told the women and children to go away and not to bother Jesus. "Can't you see that he is busy? Why are you interrupting him? He is talking to this important group of men."

Jesus, who was right there and heard everything, said, "Let the children come to me. Don't try to stop them. The kingdom of God belongs to little children. In fact, think about this and remember it: To be part of the kingdom of God, you need to come to me like these little children are—loving, trusting, and accepting."

What did Jesus mean? He meant many things. Jesus loves children, both little and big. Jesus likes childlike faith and trust and belief. He liked it that the children were excited just to see him and to be near him. They did not have to ask the kinds of questions that the men were asking. The men were suspicious and did not know whether to trust Jesus' answers. Jesus meant that he wanted to be accepted and believed. He wanted to be loved the way the children loved him. He meant that now, at the very age that you are, is a good time to love him. Do you?

   Activity: Place the coin in the glass. Have an adult try to reach the coin without tipping the glass. Then have a child do the same. Discuss the fact that sometimes children can do things that big people cannot.

25

Zacchaeus

Scripture: When Jesus came to that place, he looked up and said to Zacchaeus, "Hurry down, Zacchaeus, because I must stay in your house today" (Luke 19:5).

Entire Text: Luke 19:1–10

Objects: Chairs.

Zacchaeus was a chief tax collector. He was very rich because in those days tax collectors were allowed to charge extra money and keep it for themselves. Do you think people liked tax collectors? No, even in this day being a tax collector does not make a person popular.

Besides being a tax collector and being rich because he cheated people, Zacchaeus was also short. He was so short that he could not see this Jesus everybody was talking about when Jesus walked in a crowd of people. So Zacchaeus thought to himself, "I would really like to get a look at Jesus. What can I do?" He looked about him and thought, "If I hurry on ahead, I can climb a tree and look down on Jesus as he passes by. I can hide in the leaves and nobody will know I am there. Great idea!"

So Zacchaeus did this. He actually got to see the well-known Jesus passing by the tree. But wait! Jesus stopped.

He looked up into the tree right at Zacchaeus. Zacchaeus was so surprised that he nearly fell out of the tree. He couldn't believe it when he heard Jesus say, "Hurry down, Zacchaeus, because I must stay in your house today."

It was a very big honor for Zacchaeus to have Jesus come to his house. In those days, when people went to someone's house, it was a special compliment. The fact that it was Jesus, whom everyone wanted to get closer to, made it even more remarkable. The people standing around Jesus grumbled and complained, "How come Jesus is going to the house of a sinner and honoring this man? That's not right."

Jesus went to Zacchaeus's house because Zacchaeus believed that Jesus was the Son of God. Salvation came to Zacchaeus and his family that day. Zacchaeus said he was sorry for taking too much money from people and that he would pay people back and give money to the poor.

Jesus still comes to the house of those who love him and want to serve him. Is Jesus in this house today?

Activity: The children can stand on chairs and pretend that they are Zacchaeus looking for Jesus, or they can designate a chair as Jesus' chair because Jesus is in their house.

26

The Widow's Gift

Scripture: "I tell you that this poor widow put more in the offering box than all the others. For the others put in what they had to spare of their riches; but she, poor as she is, put in all she had—she gave all she had to live on" (Mark 12:43–44).

Entire Text: Mark 12:41–44

Object: Money.

One day Jesus was at the temple in the place where people came to give their money. It was called the treasury of the temple. It was in a courtyard with thirteen big pillars. By each pillar stood a chest. The opening of each chest was shaped like a trumpet. The people came to drop their offerings into the trumpet-shaped openings in the chests.

Jesus saw rich men giving large amounts of money. Then he saw a widow who was very poor. In those days, if your husband died, you had nobody to take care of you. Women didn't go to work for money. They had to rely on people giving them things. Life was very difficult if your husband died and you could not find another man to marry. This woman gave two mites, which is less than a penny, but it was all she had. She was very kind and unselfish. She felt that her little bit of money, when put together with the rest, might do some good.

Jesus was watching the people give their money. Who do you think Jesus felt gave the most? It was not the rich people who gave their extra money that they did not really need. It was the poor widow who gave the little she had to live on. Jesus said that she gave more than anybody else.

Many times Jesus had told the people that it was better to be poor and happy and trust in God than to be rich and have a lot of things to look after and worry about. Jesus was very pleased with the little bit that the poor widow gave. Would Jesus be happy with what you give to his church?

Activity: Give the children money. Discuss what they will give to the church or to poor people. Giving children money and helping them decide what to contribute can be more meaningful than giving children money to put in the offering plate.

27

Jesus Is My Light

Scripture:

Let us be bold, then, and say,
"The Lord is my helper,
I will not be afraid.
What can anyone do to me?" (Heb. 13:6).

Entire Text: Hebrews 13:5–8

Object: Flashlight.

When you go outside at night and it is very dark, what would help you find your way? If the electricity goes off and you need to find something, what would help you see to find what you need? If it is dark in your bedroom and you don't want to turn on the lights, what would help you see well enough to keep from bumping into things? If you have to go down in the basement and the lights are not working, what would help you not to be afraid? A candle could blow out, but a trusty flashlight could help you do all these things.

A flashlight can help you by guiding you in dark places. Think of Jesus as your flashlight. Trusting in him to guide you and following the light of his love will help you walk through the scary places of life.

When you have lost something, a flashlight can help you find it. Think of Jesus as your flashlight. When you have lost a friend, showing that friend kindness through the light of Jesus' love can help you be friends again.

When you are afraid that you will bump into things, a flashlight will light the way. Loving Jesus and following his light will keep you from doing things you will be sorry about later. It will show you when something is not good to do, like lying, stealing, or being unkind. Then you will walk in the light of Jesus rather than stumbling in the dark.

When you walk alone in the darkness, a flashlight will give you comfort. You can shine it on what frightens you and then you will not be afraid. Our verse says, "The Lord is my helper, I will not be afraid." Jesus is your flashlight, your helper. With him you do not need to be afraid.

Activity: Let the children use the flashlight and talk about how Jesus is their light and their helper.

28

Forgiveness

Scripture: Be tolerant with one another and forgive one another whenever any of you has a complaint against someone else. You must forgive one another just as the Lord has forgiven you (Col. 3:13).

Entire Text: Colossians 3:12–17

Objects: A jar or cup of dried beans, dried peas, or candy. The number represents the number of times we must forgive.

We are the people of God. He loves us and chose us. We love him and chose him to be in our lives. Therefore, there are certain things that are expected of us. We are expected to be kind to each other. Are we kind to each other? We are expected to love each other. Do we love each other? We are expected to be patient and gentle with each other. Are we patient and gentle with each other?

Because we are human, we make mistakes. When we do something wrong, we say we are sorry. We must also do something else if we are Christians. We must forgive each other. When we say we are sorry and mean it, the other person must forgive. We must forgive others just as Jesus forgives us. If our toy is broken or our feelings are hurt, it is not easy to forgive. Even then, however, Jesus wants us to forgive.

Surely, we only need to forgive a certain number of times and then the person is not allowed to do anything wrong anymore, right? That's not the way it works. We need to forgive and keep forgiving as many or more times than there are grains of sugar in the sugar bowl.

What happens if you don't forgive? The person who is unforgiven feels bad, but you feel worse. You cannot forget about what has happened and be friends with that person again. Sometimes people get angry or upset over something that happened, and they stay that way the rest of their lives. They dislike each other when they could be friends.

It is especially important that we forgive people in our family. We live each day together, and it is easy for one of us to do something to hurt or upset another. Jesus wants us to forgive as soon as the person says he or she is sorry. Do we always forgive each other?

Activity: Take turns taking an object out of the jar and telling of a time someone in the family forgave someone else.

29

Let Your Light Shine

Scripture: No one lights a lamp and puts it under a bowl; instead he puts it on the lampstand, where it gives light for everyone in the house. In the same way your light must shine before people, so that they will see the good things you do and praise your Father in heaven (Matt. 5:15–16).

Entire Text: Matthew 5:14–16

Objects: One or more candles and a bowl that will fit over a lighted candle. (It may be necessary to shorten a candle.) Candles can represent the sizes of family members. Light the candles before reading the story.

While Jesus was walking on the earth as a man, he told the people many stories and taught them much about loving God and living the life of a Christian. He taught them how to pray. He taught them how to be happy. He taught them about kindness and patience. He taught them to be humble and righteous and to do good things for other people.

Jesus also told them that they would be his witnesses. Crowds followed Jesus wherever he went, and he talked to the people, but Jesus knew he would not be living on the earth for much longer. He knew it would be up to the people who loved him to tell everyone about him when he was no longer walking on the earth. So he told the people that they were like candles.

He said that just as a candle can light a room, they would be the light for the whole world. Look closely at the candle flame. Imagine that Jesus is telling you that you are like this bright, lively flame that will shine to the world.

Jesus also said that no one lights a candle and puts a bowl over it. Look what happens when we do that. You cannot see much light. The flame on the candle will also go out because it will not have enough oxygen to burn. If you are like a candle that is hidden under a bowl, it means that God gave you a flame but you are hiding it so that nobody can see it. The light you shine for Jesus will go out.

When he said that his people are like candles, he also said that your light and my light must shine so that everyone around can see the kind and loving things we do and praise our Father in heaven. When you come into a darkened room and a candle is burning, you look at it right away. That's what we should be like. We should be cheerful and helpful. We should love God and each other. We should do kind things for each other and for other people. When we do this, our faces are shining. People notice that there is something special about us. They notice that we are Christians. They see that being a Christian is a good thing and they want to know Christ too. Are you a light shining for Jesus?

Activity: Use the candles as the story is read.

30

The Last Supper

Scripture: While they were eating, Jesus took a
piece of bread, gave a prayer of thanks, broke it,
and gave it to his disciples. "Take it," he said, "this
is my body" (Mark 14:22).

Entire Text: Mark 14:12–26

Objects: Bread (preferably a pita) and grape juice.

It was almost time for the Jews to celebrate the
Passover. Every year they remembered the time when
they were slaves in Egypt and they had to kill a lamb
and put its blood on their doorposts. Every family with
blood on its doorpost was spared from having its old-
est child die. After that happened, the people were able
to leave the country and not be slaves anymore.

Jesus' disciples asked him where they should go to
prepare the Passover meal. He told two men what to do.
He said they should go into the city of Jerusalem, where
a man carrying a jar of water would meet them. Jesus
said to follow the man until he went into a house. Then
they were to find the owner of the house and ask him
where the room was that Jesus and his disciples were to
use when they ate the Passover meal. To you and me
this may sound like a strange thing to do. These men,
however, had been surprised so many times by the mir-

acles and wonderful things that Jesus had already done that they followed his instructions.

When they found the owner and asked him where the room was, he showed them to a large upstairs room with a table big enough for Jesus and the twelve disciples. The two disciples got everything they needed.

When Jesus and the rest of the disciples arrived, they all sat down to eat. It was a special meal for Jesus because he knew it would be his last on earth. While they were eating, Jesus took a piece of flat bread and said a prayer. Then he broke off a piece of the bread for each disciple, for this bread is usually broken and not cut. He said to the disciples, "This is my body." Jesus knew that he was about to have his body killed, or broken.

Then Jesus took a cup of drink. Again he gave a short prayer. Jesus handed it to the disciples and they all drank from the cup. Then Jesus said, "This is my blood which is poured out for many." Jesus knew they would put nails in his hands and pierce his side with a spear, and he would bleed. The disciples must have wished Jesus would not talk this way. Then they all sang a hymn and went out to the Mount of Olives.

Why did Jesus do this with his disciples? He wanted to give them a ceremony, like the Passover, to remember him. He wanted them to think often about how he died for their sins. We have two names for this time to remember. We call it the Lord's Supper because it was the Lord's last and special supper where he showed the disciples what to do. We also call it communion because we are together with others who love Jesus, and we feel close to Jesus. We can do this as a family.

Activity: Use the bread and grape juice as you have a family communion.

Sheryl Bruinsma is a Springfield, Pennsylvania, teacher who has taught for over thirty years and recently earned her Ed.D. degree. This is her eighth object lesson book.